GARY JONES

New York

Contents

Introduction   iv

New York, A History   1

When to Go   11

Getting Around   15

Where to Stay   27

Where to Eat   31

What to Visit   36

Museums   45

Art Galleries   52

Coffee Shops   57

Bars   62

Nightclubs   66

Only in New York   69

Safety Tips   76

Recommended Travel Itinerary   78

Conclusion   89

Thank You   91

Introduction

This book contains everything you need to know for a three-day trip to New York. But make no mistake — this travel guide does not simply hand you a list of sights to see and places to visit. It is more than that.

I encourage you to fully engage with this book, learn the stories of the sights and the preface of the places. Then, when you get to New York, I urge you to remember what you learned in order to fully fall in love with this great city.

More practically, this book contains the basic things you need to know before making the trip. It starts with New York's history, how it was built and what it has to offer now. Then, it answers the realistic questions: When should you go? What should you bring? Where should you stay? I hope you'll be pleased to know that New York City has every option possible for every kind of tourist.

Now, the fun begins. In the succeeding chapters, I offer you the key to the city and its endless list of restaurants, sights, museums, art galleries, coffee shops, bars, and nightclubs. Each item on the list presents a unique experience, although no list can truly encapsulate New York. I can only hope that this book gives you a taste of New York, and that it inspires you to be brave enough to take a bite of the Big Apple.

Thanks for downloading this book, I hope you enjoy it!

1

New York, A History

New York is a city of superlatives. It is America's crown jewel — it is the most populated, most expensive, and most famous city in the US, and understandably so. New York is the quintessential American city — the glamour, ambition, and ideals of New York are born from the glamour, ambition, and ideals of America itself. But New York hasn't always been the magnificent metropolis that it is now.

In the early 1600s, a new land had just begun to take shape, and the rest of the world had started to notice. Back then, New York City was a patch of lush, green land purchased by the Dutch West India Company for 60 gold coins. It had a meager population of 5,000. For the city to have value, it needed enough settlers to inhabit, work, and defend the land. Attracting settlers proved to be difficult: The Dutch's hold on New York was fragile and the threat of Indian War was discouraging. Eventually, the Dutch failed to defend New York, so they surrendered the city to British invaders.

The British, bringing their slaves and businesses, proceeded to make New York a center of slavery and trading. The new land became a symbol of economic and religious freedom, attracting German and English immigrants. New York flourished, and by 1790, it had a population of 340,000, surpassing even that of Philadelphia's.

Several more events in history facilitated the influx of immigrants to New York — most notably, the end of America's revolutionary war, the Irish potato famine, and the abolition of slavery. About 380,000 German, Irish, and African migrants flocked to the new land. New York soon became America's immigration gateway, welcoming over 8 million immigrants by 1857.

New York ,Manhattan ,1870

Never before has the world witnessed the emergence of a promised land where one is welcomed despite status, color, or wealth. It prompted the coining of the term "melting pot," inspiring a play of the same name. In the play, it elevated America to "God's crucible," and that the country was to serve the same purpose of a melting pot. It painted the picture of millions of immigrants gathered in Ellis Island. As told by the play, America is a quilt of people with different loyalties, languages, and cultures; and that to build a nation, they would have to set aside their differences. A peaceful, harmonious, productive co-existence embodies God's ideal of America.

New York has always been the epitome of the American dream. It values individual merit, collective diversity, and universal freedom. The city effectively sells the idea that with hard work, you can be anything you want to be. New York is the product of the blood, sweat, and tears of immigrants. It is the collective effort of every man and woman who has ever hoped, dreamed, and worked.

Today, New York remains a land of possibilities and adventure. Each of its five boroughs — Manhattan, Brooklyn, Queens, Bronx, and Staten Island — offers a distinct, unparalleled experience.

MANHATTAN

Times Square. Central Park. Empire State Building. Think of New York, and you will most likely come up with an image straight out of Manhattan's skyline. Not only is it the most recognizable of the five boroughs, it is also the richest, most famous, and most densely

4

populated. Manhattan is the brains, the money, and the dazzle of New York. Here are some of the many things that the city can offer:

World's largest stock exchanges (New York Stock Exchange, NASDAQ)

World's largest museums (Solomon R. Guggenheim, Metropolitan Museum
of Art, American Museum of Natural History, Whitney Museum of American Art, Museum of Modern Art)

Prestigious universities (Cornell Tech, Columbia University, New York University, and Rockefeller University)

Famous works of architecture and landmarks (Chrysler Building, One World Trade Center, Grand Central Terminal)

Media and entertainment (Carnegie Hall, Broadway, Rockefeller Center)

BROOKLYN

If Manhattan is the overachieving firstborn, Brooklyn is the creative middle child. This is not to undermine Brooklyn's status as an industrial city. Rather, it is to acknowledge that its strength isn't its economy, but its culture.

Its residents are ethnically diverse — in fact, over half of its population are Jewish, Chinese, African-American, Latino, and Muslim. In recent years, Brooklyn struggled with gentrification. As Manhattan residential prices skyrocketed, those who cannot afford the city moved to Brooklyn, its cheaper counterpart. Rent in Brooklyn skyrocketed in turn.

Today, Brooklyn is the "it" place. It has become a hub for art, technology, food, live music, and sports.

Here are some of Brooklyn's prized jewels:

Art galleries and museums (Brooklyn Museum, Smack Mellon Gallery, Brooklyn Art Space)

Happy hours and live music (Saint Vitus, The Bell House, Hank's Saloon, Montero's Bar)

Food scene (Vinegar Hill House, Cafe Esencia, Brooklyn Pizza)

Coney Island (Wonder Wheel, The Cyclone, Coney Island Beach)

QUEENS

One of New York's greatest misfortunes is Little Italy. Once a bustling food hub populated by Italian-American immigrants, Little Italy has become too expensive for the very people that shaped it to be the destination that it is now. The result is a gimmicky tourist trap selling Italian aesthetic without Italian authenticity.

Queens, on the other hand, kept and owned its uniqueness. Owing to its dominant population of Asian, Latino, and African American, Queens has an innate, self-realized cultural identity born from being a true melting pot. Its cultural innovation does not look for inspiration from Brooklyn and Manhattan. Rather, Queens' art, food, and music scene are the result of ingenious authenticity.

It often gets overshadowed by its more famous neighbors, but not anymore. In 2015, it topped Lonely Planet's list as the best travel destination in the United States. Here's why:

Modern art scene (Long Island graffiti, Queens Museum, Museum of Modern Art PS1)

Unique, authentic culinary identity (I Love Paraguay, Sami's Kabab House, Peking BBQ, Jeaw Hon New York)

Up-and-coming microbreweries (Mikkeller, Finback Brewery, Bridge and Tunnel Brewery)

BRONX

In the 1970s, many Bronx residents experienced unlivable conditions — lack of security, state-sponsored redlining, and extreme poverty. These factors meant that compared to other boroughs, Bronx hasn't been given a fair fight. The government's efforts for rehabilitation have stalled; meanwhile, people were still living in Dickensian conditions. So, with its characteristic hustle, Bronx took matters into its own hands.

Bronx is the birthplace of hip-hop. Its mellifluous, often humorous political poeticism, punctuated by rhythm and beats, forced the city to listen to a marginalized group that it has repeatedly failed. What began as a musical, cultural self-expression took the boroughs, the city, and the world by storm. In 2017, hip-hop was a $10-billion-a-year industry.

Bronx's cultural achievements inspired a recent wave of rehabilitation, attracting more and more tourists. Here's what they come for:

Famous family-friendly tourist spots (Bronx Zoo, New York Botanical Garden, Crotona Park, Joyce Kilmer Park, Poe Cottage)

Baseball (NY Yankees Baseball, Yankees Stadium)

Art (Bronx Museum of the Arts, Bronx Graffiti Art Gallery, Lehman Center for the Performing Arts)

Neighborhoods (Zero Otto Nove, Arthur Avenue, Belmont)

STATEN ISLAND

Staten Island may have a small, unassuming population, but its attractions are so steeped with history and cultural value that you'd be remiss to not visit it. Hitch a free ride on the Staten Island ferry and begin to explore this quaint hidden gem.

Parks and wildlife (Willowbrook Park, Freshkills Parks, High Rock Park, Gateway National Recreation)

View from the ferry (New York Harbor, Statue of Liberty)

Museums (September 11 Memorial, National Lighthouse Museum,

Staten Island Museum, Alice Austen House)

2

When to Go

New York is worth seeing any day of the year, but some months are more challenging than others. New York's calendar dramatically dictates the weather, experience, and prices you're going to get. Plan your trip strategically to see the New York you want to see.

January - March

The average high is 39F°, and the average low is 26°F. December may be over, but winter is well underway. Expect snow, rain, or sleet.

Dress warmly — pack your boots, gloves, scarves, socks, coats, and jackets. Towards the end of March, the weather should get warmer in preparation for spring.

If a freezing New York winter doesn't bother you, visit the city during these months. By now, the Christmas tourists will have gone home, and you'll have the city to yourself. The lines are shorter and the airfare is cheaper. You are also more likely to get easier reservations on hotels, restaurants, and Broadway tickets.

April - July

The average high is 70°F, and the average low is 45°F. Spring comes with some heavy rain at first, but after a few weeks, the sky should clear up. Be prepared for rain or shine. Think layers: Bring a light jacket, pullovers, long sleeves, breathable shirt, and sweaters.

The cold, rainy nights may be over, but spring comes with a torrent of tourists. April to July is peak season: The sights are crowded, hotel prices are high, and it is near impossible to visit attractions without a previous booking.

August - October

The average high is 74°F, and the average low is 60°F. Next to spring, fall is the most strategic time to visit New York. School starts in September, which means that there are fewer locals and tourists out on the street. On top of that, the weather becomes more agreeable the closer you get to October. Hotel and airfare prices come at a bargain, too.

August and September are still accompanied by light rain, but in October, the crisp, cool breeze welcomes you. Take this opportunity to explore the city. Make sure to pack layers, light coats, and comfortable shoes.

November - December

The average high is 49°F, and the average low is 36°F. New York's winter is brutally cold and dark — in fact, the city only sees 6 hours of daylight. But winter has its perks, too. For one, a year-end visit in New York doesn't hurt the eyes. Towards the end of the year, the city turns into a picturesque winter wonderland.

The winter also brings fun activities — Macy's Thanksgiving parade, tree-lighting in Rockefeller Center, ice-skating in Bryant Park, and the New Year countdown in Times Square, to name a few.

Be prepared for the cold, rain, and snow. Bring hats, scarves, gloves, jackets, sweaters, umbrellas, and boots.

George Washington Bridge

3

Getting Around

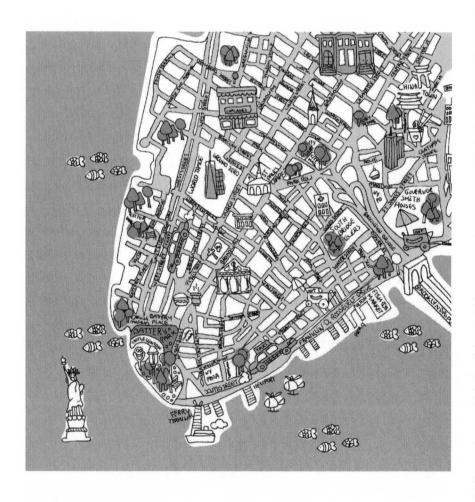

Getting to New York

New York has two main international airports: John F. Kennedy (Jamaica, Queens) and LaGuardia (Jackson Heights, Queens). There are three factors to consider when choosing an airport: price, reliability, and distance.

https://www.jfkairport.com/

https://www.laguardiaairport.com/

PRICE: Airfare costs are subject to many factors like oil prices, cost competition, and weather conditions. These factors are unrelated to the airport.

While airfare is unpredictable, taxi fare is not. Taxis at JFK have a flat rate of $52.50, while LaGuardia's metered taxis cost $40, plus toll.

RELIABILITY: According to the US Department of Transportation, LaGuardia flights are most likely to be delayed, and on some occasions, cancelled. In 2015, only 73% of arrivals were on time, compared to JFK's 77%.

DISTANCE: LaGuardia is 8.6 miles away from Midtown Manhattan, compared to JFK's 14.7.

Getting around New York

New York City is densely populated and heavily visited; in fact, over 4.1 million people come to and from the city every day. New York's straightforward grid system makes it navigable, but a city with so many people can only contain so many private cars. Luckily, public transportation is inexpensive, efficient, and effective.

Subway/Metro

The New York City Subway is the most convenient way to commute to and from Manhattan, Brooklyn, Queens, and Bronx. It is, however, a complex system and is a common source of frustration for newcomers. Here's a quick guide to using the subway.

Buy a Metro card. It has two variants: pay-per-ride and unlimited. An unlimited card costs $32 and is valid for 7 days. To get the best value for your money, only choose this option if you intend to take 15-20 rides. Otherwise, stick to the reloadable pay-per-ride cards.

Some subway stations can be hard to find. To find a station, simply look for tall globe lamps. Green lamps are entrances and red ones are exits.

Check the station sign. The name of the station is written in large, white letters. The color-coded circles or diamonds indicates the route. For example, a subway sign with a yellow icon lettered N, Q, R, or W has a route that takes the Broadway line.

New York Subway Phone: 511

http://web.mta.info/maps/submap.html

Follow this legend:

Red icons numbered 1, 2, 3 - Broadway - 7th Street

Green icons numbered 4, 5, 6 - Lexington Ave.

Purple icons numbered 7 - Flushing

Blue icons lettered A, C, E - 8th Avenue

Orange icons lettered B, D, F, M - 6th Avenue

Brown icons lettered J, Z - Nassau Street

Grey icon lettered L - Canarsie

Check that you're riding towards the right direction before swiping your Metro card at the turnstile. If you're at the wrong platform and you've already swiped, you can't get a refund. You also have to wait for a minimum of 18 minutes before you can swipe again. Hold the Metro Card with the logo and magnetic strip facing you, and then swipe away from you. Once you hear a click, you can go ahead and push the turnstile.

Follow the black subway signs to find the right platform for your train. You will see a sign that says "local" or "express." Local trains have drop-offs at every stop, while express trains have select stops. Beginners are recommended to take the local train.

Wait for the train. Allow exiting passengers to clear off before stepping in.
Wait for your stop, and then exit to the platform.

Bus

Buses are slower than subways, but they are also suitable for sightseeing and if you're traveling with kids. Simply wait at designated bus stops, flag down the bus, and hop in. You can either use a Metro Card or pay with cash. When you reach your stop, pull the stop cord. Wait for the bus to stop, and then go to the exit at the back of the bus.

Taxi and apps

Cars are generally not recommended for tourists because of costly parking and heavy traffic, but taxis and ride-share apps are widely used. Taxis are a New York institution, but Grab, Lyft, and Uber are considered safer. However, price surge is a concern for most — in times of high demand, rush hours, and emergencies, these apps charge up to double the original fare.

Ferry

As you may have noticed, New York's subway system extends to all boroughs except Staten Island. To get there, you need to take the ferry. On weekdays, a ferry departs from Whitehall Terminal, Manhattan to St. George, Staten Island every 30 minutes. The ferry is free, efficient, and always open.

https://www.ferry.nyc/

Notes

The Metropolitan Transportation Authority (MTA) has a free app available for download on Android and iOS devices. It contains schedules of subway stops, trains, and buses. It also has a feature that allows you to see the easiest route from one place to another.

Before riding, learn how to read and interpret subway maps, terminologies and symbols. You can grab a free subway map at ticket booths.

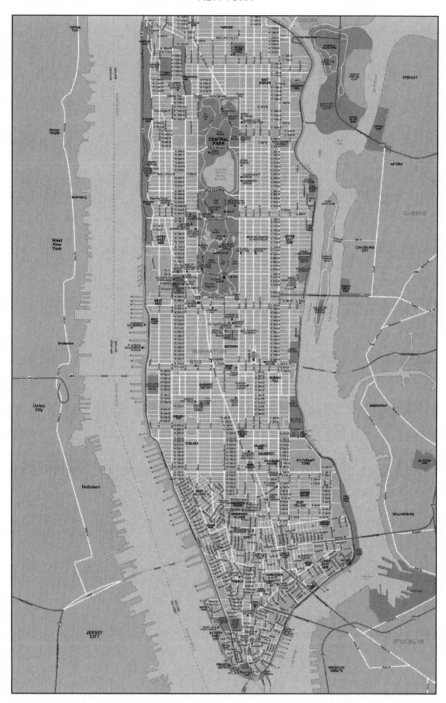

Manhattan

Brooklyn Map

Queens Map

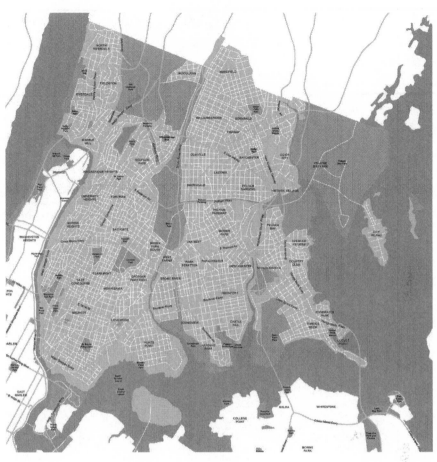

Bronx

Staten Island

4

Where to Stay

A quick Internet search of hotel room prices can be overwhelming because of New York's accommodation prices. In fact, a 25-sqm room in a Manhattan hotel chain averages at $450 per night. But visiting

New York doesn't always have to break the bank. You just have to know where to look.

Nowadays, you have a plethora of options — home rentals, dormitories, bed and breakfasts, capsule hotels, hostels, and no-frill hotels. Listed below are the top five accommodations in New York City.

5. U.S. Pacific Hotel (Chinatown)
(106 Bowery 2FL, Chinatown, New York City)

Right at the heart of Chinatown, five minutes from the subway, 20 from the Brooklyn Bridge. All for $60 a night.

The U.S. Pacific Hotel is for the unfussy traveler. An economy room in this hotel is clean and small, prioritizing function over form. It has a double bed, air-conditioning, TV, shared bathroom, and free WiFi.

This hotel is recommended for tourists who are simply looking for a place to sleep, take a shower, and spend the rest of the trip out in the city.

Phone:+1 212-226-0300

4. The Queens Hotel (Queens)
(65-15 Queens Boulevard, Queens, NY)

The Queens Hotel is conveniently located near public parks, Grand Central Station, Empire State Building, and the LaGuardia airport.

At $120 per night, you get a clean, simple room with a slight hint of luxury — air-conditioning, flat-screen TV, private bathroom, free continental breakfast, and more space than you would find in most New

York hotel rooms.

The Queens Hotel is for the traveler who wants to (sensibly) splurge on themselves.

Phone:+1 718-458-8808

3. Harlem Lofts (Harlem)
(33 West 128th Street 1, Harlem, New York City)

Some people just want to see the sights, but others want to live like a local. Harlem Lofts, a group of centrally located rental apartments in Harlem, aims to show you authentic New York living.

It is accessible by public transport and is a stone's throw away from the National Jazz Museum, Central Park, Yankee Stadium, and Columbia University.

At $130 per night, you get a spacious studio apartment with a fully functional kitchen, large double bed, flat-screen TV, free WiFi, and a patio. Oh, and it offers a spectacular garden view, too.

Phone: +1 212-280-8866

2. Hotel RL by Red Lion Brooklyn (Brooklyn)
(1080 Broadway, Bed-Stuy, Brooklyn, NY)

Hotel RL is a 3-star hotel located in Bedstuy, Brooklyn. It is close to public transportation, restaurants, flea markets, and parks.

A night's stay in Hotel RL's queen room costs $100. The room is larger than most hotels at the same price point, and it has air-conditioning, heating, flat-screen TV, and private bathroom.

The hotel also offers free WiFi, disability access, game rooms, and laundry facilities. It even allows pets!

Hotel RL is for the adventurous traveler interested in seeing the sights off the beaten path. The pomps and frills of Manhattan are distant, dimmed by the brilliance of Brooklyn's vibrant art, music, and nightlife.

Phone: +1 718-715-4850

1. Broadway Hotel & Hostel (Upper West Side)

(230 West 101 Street, Upper West Side, New York City,)

Broadway Hotel & Hostel is for the smart, budget-minded traveler. The hotel is strategically located — it is far enough from the franticness of Times Square, yet close enough to famous tourist spots like Central Park, Rockefeller Center, and the Metropolitan Museum of Art.

Public transportation options, like the subway and bus, are also accessible from the hotel.

A night at Broadway Hotel costs $80 for two people. The double room is complete with basic amenities like air-conditioning, heating, flat-screen TV, private bathroom, and free WiFi. The hotel has convenient common areas, too; it has a library, theatre room, dining room, and guest kitchen.

Phone: +1 212-865-7710

5

Where to Eat

With diverse cultures come diverse cuisines. How diverse, you say? As of 2018, New York City has 26,700 restaurants. To comprehend this number, take this situation: Say you eat at a different restaurant for breakfast, lunch, and dinner every day.

It would take you 24 years to get through all the restaurants in New York. That's not even including informal food trucks, hotdog vendors, and halal stands.

New York is a foodie's gastronomic heaven. If you only have 72 hours to feast, here are the top five restaurants you can't miss.

5. Le Coucou

Traveling is as good a time as any to indulge in a little taste of luxury. When indulging in New York, do it in Le Coucou. This upscale French restaurant has a classic, elegant decor worthy of one of the top fine dining restaurants in New York. What sets it apart is its chef, Daniel Rose.

Like all fine dining restaurants, the prices are sky-high, the menu is unpronounceable, yet the dress code is casual and the servers are warm and down-to-earth. Rose took the snobbery and pretense away from French cuisine and let the food stand on its own merits.

Le Coucou is open every day of the week from 7 a.m. to 2 p.m., and from 5 p.m. to 11 p.m. It is located at 138 Lafayette St., New York 10013.

Phone:+1 212-271-4252

https://lecoucou.com/

4. Agern

Modern culture sees food as an adventure, and this philosophy is very much evident in Agern. This seasonal Scandinavian restaurant is for the brave foodie who goes for the wildest, most unusual thing in the menu.

In Agern, the food is innovative and exciting, yet it retains familiar ingredients.

On top of the unique dining experience, Agern is located at Grand Central Terminal. This hidden gem, however, is situated away from the rushing commuters. Its secluded atmosphere gives the feeling that you are on the verge of discovery — a gastronomical discovery, at that.

Take a leap of faith. Visit Agern in Grand Central Terminal, 89 E 42nd St., New York 10017, anytime from 11:30 a.m. to 2:30 p.m., and 5:30 p.m. to 10 p.m. The restaurant is open every day except Sunday.

Phone: +1 646-568-4018

http://agernrestaurant.com/

3. Sotto Casa Pizzeria

When it comes to pizza, New York has made a name for itself; and Sotto Casa happens to be the most important name on the list. Known as the highest-rated restaurant in the city, this restaurant serves authentic Italian food made from fresh Neapolitan ingredients. Its most famous dishes are Diavola pie and margherita pizza, best paired with a glass of rose.

Sotto Casa literally translates to "under home," which accurately captures the warm, cozy feel of the restaurant. It feels like somebody's Italian grandmother's home. It shows not only in the food and vibe, but the service, too.

Sotto Casa has two locations: 298 Atlantic Avenue, Brooklyn, New York 11201, and 227 Lenox Avenue, Harlem, New York 10027. Both branches are open from 5 p.m. to 10:30 p.m.

Phone:+1 646-928-4870

http://www.sottocasanyc.com/harlem/

2. Los Tacos No.1

Los Tacos is unlike anything on this list. It doesn't have the pomps and frills of fine dining; it doesn't even have seating. But you're in New York, and any trip without good old-fashioned street food is incomplete.

Los Tacos is a hidden treasure. What gives it away is the long line that always forms in front of it. Regulars come for their fresh-baked corn tortilla and slow-cooked adobado, bathed in copious amounts of roasted salsa.

Los Tacos has two locations. One is in 229 W 43rd St., New York, NY 10036, only a few steps away from Times Square. The other is located at 75 9th Ave., New York, NY 10011, close to Chelsea Market. Both branches are open every day from 11 a.m. 10 p.m.

Phone:+1 212-256-0343

https://www.lostacos1.com/

1. Blue Hill

Blue Hill is a family-owned restaurant notable for its farm-to-table ethos. Its owner, founder, and chef Dan Barber aims for a holistic fine dining experience unlike any other. According to him, the farmer's task has always been focused on producing quantity or yields, not quality or taste. Barber sees this as a problem, and he got to the root of it.

The Blue Hill Restaurant is a product of good, ethical farming and cooking. The menu often rotates, depending on which crop is abundant. Do try their world-famous carrot steak, when available.

The restaurant has two locations, only one of which is in New York City. Blue Hill New York is at 75 Washington Pl New York, NY 10011. It is open every day from 5 p.m. to 11 p.m.

Phone: 212 539 0959

https://www.bluehillfarm.com/dine/new-york

6

What to Visit

New York City has some of the most recognizable sights in the world — Brooklyn Bridge, Times Square, Empire State Building, to name a few. Its iconic landmarks are telling of the ideals that the city stands for. The Statue of Liberty, gifted by France to celebrate America's successful revolution, signifies hope and freedom for all.

The Wall Street Charging Bull, installed two years after the 1987 stock market crash, symbolizes the fierce resilience and strength of the American people. The One World Trade Center stands to always honor its twin's absence in the Manhattan skyline.

These magnificent landmarks come with an equally magnificent history of New York and its people.

Here are five attractions you can't miss.

5. Empire State Building

This iconic 102-story building was completed in 1931. At the time of its completion, it was the tallest building in the world. The Empire State Building is home to 25,000 businesses and 20,000 tenants; its unusually large capacity meant that the building even has its own zip code.

Empire State Building

Following New York's financial boom in the 1920s, this building, along with Chrysler and Bank of Manhattan, were competing entries in a contest to build the world's largest skyscraper. The Empire State Building was completed in a record-breaking 20 months, winning the contest and retaining its throne until 1931.

The 86th and 102nd floor of the building are observation decks open 365 days a year from 8 a.m. to 2 a.m., with an admission fee of $57 for adults, $51 for children, and $55 for seniors. New York's landmarks are visible from the top, including the Statue of Liberty, Brooklyn Bridge, Yankee Stadium, Chrysler Building, United Nations, and Rockefeller Park.

http://www.esbnyc.com/

4. 9/11 Memorial

Every New Yorker remembers where they were when they heard the terrible news. On the fateful morning of September 11, 2001, 2,977 people lost their lives to terrorism. Never before has there been a terrorist attack of such scale, and in Manhattan, no less.

The impact was massive — one out of five New Yorkers knew someone who was injured or killed in the attack. One out of five lost a parent, a child, a sibling, or a friend. The 9/11 Memorial seeks to remember, with love and kindness, all the valuable lives that the city lost to fear and hatred.

9/11 Memorial

Perhaps the most notable installment of the memorial museum is the Reflecting Absence, a 16-acre pool with twin waterfalls. Its sides are inscripted with the names of its casualties. It is the largest, most expensive public memorial in the US. New York is a city that draws your eyes upwards; Reflecting Absence forces you to look down in remembrance and contemplation.

The September 11 Memorial Museum is open every day from 7:30 a.m. to 9 p.m. Admission tickets cost $24 for adults, $20 for seniors, and $15 for children. This fee is waived for family members of the victims.

https://www.911memorial.org/

3. Central Park

In mid-1800s, New York was becoming a highly urbanized city; so much so that to take a break from the hustle and bustle of the city, people visited cemeteries, as they were one of the few open spaces available to the public. Architect Andrew Jackson Downing and poet William Cullen Bryant proposed and publicized the need for a public park. It was, at the time, a revolution that appealed to civic-mindedness, community, and democracy.

These men aimed to build a park for the people, and they succeeded.

Central Park

Today, Central Park is one of New York's top attractions, seeing over 42 million people per year. Every day, almost 110,000 people take a shade under any one of its 26,000 trees. It is located between the Upper West

Side and the Upper East Side, making it New York's oasis. It is home to a zoo, museum, lake, ice-skating rink, castle, playground, fountains, bridges, and numerous food stalls.

Central Park is open every day from 6 a.m. to 1 a.m. Admission is free for everyone.

http://www.centralparknyc.org/

2. Brooklyn Bridge

Brooklyn Bridge made history by being the first hybrid bridge and the tallest man-made structure at the time of its construction. It prompted the merging of the two most populated industrial boroughs in New York — Brooklyn and Manhattan.

The Brooklyn Bridge, like most of New York's infrastructures, was built by immigrants who were paid to work in unsafe conditions for less than $2 per hour. Over two dozen people died during the construction of this bridge, but despite its bleak history, the end result was a sensation. As it was the first suspension bridge of its kind, there were many doubts to its safety and reliability. These doubts were put to rest by P.T. Barnum in 1884, when he crossed the bridge with 12 elephants.

Today, the engineering feat that is Brooklyn Bridge has many accolades to its laurel. It is considered the eighth wonder of the world, a National Historic landmark, and a National Historic Civil Engineering Landmark.

Brooklyn Bridge

The Brooklyn Bridge is a 25-minute walk from Brooklyn to Manhattan. It is open 24/7, free of charge. It has a panoramic view of New York, Brooklyn, and the Statue of Liberty.

1. Times Square

Appearing in countless films, shows, books, and music videos, Times Square is the most recognizable landmark of New York. The intersection of Broadway, 7th Avenue, and 42nd Street is the epitome of bright lights, big city: flashing neon lights, gigantic billboards, and bustling crowds. Times Square is home to countless retail stores, Broadway theatres, Hard Rock Cafe, the New York Times, and more.

Times Square is open 24/7. At its center is a traffic-free section with chairs and tables, where people can sit, talk, drink coffee, and watch the fast-paced world go by. Visit Times Square at midnight, when the sky is dark and the crowd has cleared. The bright neon lights bounce off passing cars and bathe the city with a kaleidoscope of colors.

https://www.timessquarenyc.org/

7

Museums

New York is inarguably a world-renowned nucleus of art and culture. Like all cities of its caliber, New York flaunts its status and achievements with museums.

What make the city's museums unique, however, are the ideals that the city itself were built upon. The poor, the tired, and the huddled masses entered the country through New York and proceeded to build a city that encouraged and respected the beauty of diversity.

The best of New York's museums reflect the city's tremendous wealth of tradition, knowledge, and history accumulated from many countries and across many generations.

5. American Museum of Natural History (Upper West Side, Manhattan)

The American Museum of Natural History (AMNH) is the largest science museum in New York, containing over 30 million specimens and artifacts. Over 5 million people visit the museum every year.

Its interactive and kid-friendly exhibits make it the top choice for family museum trips. AMNH has 45 permanent exhibit halls dedicated to insects, birds, reptiles, amphibians, mammals, dinosaur fossils, trees, and more. The museum's most visited attraction is the Hayden Planetarium, whose dome is the exact replica of the night sky as seen from Earth.

American Museum Of Natural History

AMNH is open every day from 10 a.m. to 5:45 p.m. The museum imposes a pay-what-you-wish admission system, but the recommended fee for adults is $22, and for senior citizens and students, $17.

Phone: 212-769-5100
https://www.amnh.org/

4. Solomon Guggenheim Museum (Upper East Side, Manhattan)

Its avant-garde architecture alone makes the Solomon Guggenheim Museum a must-see for every tourist. Designed by Frank Lloyd Wright in 1959, the striking cyclical exterior marked a revolutionary art movement that symbolized the coming of the 20th century.

The museum's dedication to modern, post-modern, and contemporary art extends to its collection, featuring works of Picasso, Kandinsky, Cezanne, Brach, Chagall, and more.

The Solomon Guggenheim Museum is open every day from 10 a.m. to 5:45 p.m. Expect large crowds on Mondays. The museum charges a fee of $25 for adults, $18 for senior citizens and students, and receives pay-what-you-wish admission fees on Saturdays.

Phone: 212 423 3500
https://www.guggenheim.org/

3. Tenement Museum (Lower East Side, Manhattan)

Modern museums have a general format: visually striking paintings, sculptures, art, and artifacts. They are attempts to preserve culture, tradition, and life — but history hasn't always been impartial. It often only shows Renaissance art and kings' tombs; it often only remembers the daring, the brilliant, and the rich.

In this respect, the Tenement Museum is the museum less traveled — it seeks to remember everyday people. Located at 97 Orchard Street in the Lower East Side, it sits in a row of tenement buildings that look exactly like it. Beneath this unassuming facade is a hidden gem. The building was built in 1863, housing over 15,000 people, almost all of which were immigrants of German, Irish, Latin American, Jewish, Italian, and Asian descent.

It was condemned in 1935; for 53 years, the tenement remained unoccupied and untouched. When the building was discovered in 1988, expert historians were able to recover details of the lives of the tenants. Evidences like personal effects, government census surveys, even changes in decor are most telling. From those, experts were able to approximate answers to questions one would ask an immigrant: why they left their country, how life was in America, and how they have affected the succeeding generations.

The Tenement Museum provides a unique, off-the-beaten-path New York experience. Admission is only available through guided 2-hour tours, which costs $25 for adults and $20 for children and senior citizens.

Phone: 212-982-8420
https://www.tenement.org/contact.html

2. The Museum of Modern Art (Midtown Manhattan)

The concept of a modern museum inspires a mental image of a white cube — that is, paintings hung on plain walls, a dynamic range of colors contrasting with a stark white background. It seems commonplace today, but it was revolutionary during its time.

Such a minimalist display fosters a sense of serenity and intimacy, allowing the viewer to engage with the art with his own context, stories, and emotions. By removing art from its original intended purposes, the viewer converses with the art on his own terms. Such is the founding principle of the Museum of Modern Art, or MoMA. Its permanent collection includes famous artworks by van Gogh, Warhol, Bacon, Dali, Gauguin, Kahlo, Matisse, and Magritte.

MoMA attracts over 3 million people per year. Its building at 11 W 53rd Street is open seven days a week from 10:30 a.m. to 5:30 p.m. Its second location, 22-25 Jackson Ave., Long Island City, NY 11101, is open every day except Tuesdays and Wednesdays, from 12 p.m. to 6 p.m. Admission tickets cost $25 for adults, $18 for seniors, and $14 for students.

https://www.moma.org/

1. The Metropolitan Museum of Art (Upper East Side, Manhattan)

The Metropolitan Museum of Art, colloquially known as The Met, is the most visited museum in New York, attracting more than 7 million visitors annually. Founded in 1870, The Met now contains 2 million permanent artworks collected from over 50 countries. The museum features art collected from Egypt, Europe, Asia, America, and even Ancient Greek and Rome.

Metropolitan Museum Of Art

Art holds the unique power of transforming people. It compels, and in some cases, forces, a shift in perspective using different styles, themes, and methods. But the most significant development in art history was not a style, theme, or method. It was a movement — specifically, the movement to grant the transformative power of art to people regardless of class, creed, or race, effectively making it a right, not a privilege.

Of all the 83 museums in New York, the Met easily ranks first in terms of quantity and diversity of artworks. But perhaps its most important quality is its accessibility — the Met and the 2 million artworks it houses are available to the general public every day, free of charge.

Phone: 212-535-7710
https://www.metmuseum.org/

8

Art Galleries

To differentiate, museums have the sole purpose of displaying art; galleries, on the other hand, display art for purchase. New York has been the cradle of many art movements, especially during the 21st century.

Here are the top five galleries you can visit if you're interested in taking home an art piece.

5. 47 Canal

47 Canal founders Margaret Lee and Oliver Newton intended the gallery space for emerging contemporary artists who pride themselves in outside-the-box thinking. Some of the gallery's artists are Michele Abeles, Alisa Baremboym, and Xavier Cha.

Visit 47 Canal in 291 Grand St, New York, NY 10002, Wednesdays through Sundays, 11 a.m. to 6 p.m.

Phone: +1 646-415-7712
http://www.47canal.us/

4. CLEARING

CLEARING focuses on the young up-and-comers of the contemporary art world. Situated in the off-the-beaten path road to Bushwick, Brooklyn, this gallery features work by artists such as Harold Ancart, Lili Reynaud-Dewar, and Marina Pinsky.

The CLEARING Gallery is located at 396 Johnson Avenue, Brooklyn, NY 11206, USA. It is open from 11 a.m. to 6 p.m. every day except Sundays and Mondays.

Phone: +1 718-456-0396
http://www.c-l-e-a-r-i-n-g.com/

3. David Zwirner Gallery

America's most powerful art dealer, David Zwirner, founded his first ever gallery in SoHo. Over the years, his gallery spaces have shown revolutionary contemporary exhibits such as Bruce Nauman (2001) and Claes Oldenburg: Early Work (2005).

David Zwirner has four spaces in the world, three of which are in New York. Before coming, call them to ask if they have an open exhibition. 525 West 19th Street, New York

Phone:+ 1 212 727 2070
https://www.davidzwirner.com/

2. Luhring Augustine Gallery

In the past 20 years, waves of modern artists moved to Chelsea because of the relatively cheap rent. With the artists came curators, dealers, and eventually, galleries.

Luhring Augustine, built in 1985, is one of the pioneer galleries of the Chelsea art scene. The gallery features works of painters, sculptors, photographers, and artists with special focus on contemporary art, like Janina Antoni, Charles Atlas, and Jason Moran.

Luhring Augustine Gallery is at 531 W 24th St, New York, NY 10011. It is open weekdays from 10 a.m. to 6 p.m.

Phone: +1 212-206-9100
http://www.luhringaugustine.com/

1. Gagosian Gallery

Larry Gagosian's gallery not only indicates, but also sets and shapes the future of modern art. This influential gallery features artists like Michael Andrews, Urs Fischer, and Elizabeth Peyton. The Gagosian is best known for the extravagant Damien Hirst exhibit in 2000, which featured 16 new sculptures. One installation in particular was notable — Love Lost, a gigantic fish tank with a gynecologist office inside it.

Gagosian Gallery has 16 locations in the world, five of which are in New York. All five are open weekdays from 10 a.m. to 6 p.m.

980 Madison Avenue, New York, NY 10075

976 Madison Avenue, New York, NY 10075

821 Park Avenue, New York, NY 10021

555 West 24th Street, New York, NY 10011

522 West 21st Street, New York, NY 10011

Phone: +1 212-741-1111
https://www.gagosian.com/

9

Coffee Shops

In New York, food and drink hypes come and go. The city has seen the rise and fall of the likes of avocado toast, unicorn-colored food, brussel sprouts, and kale smoothies. Everything comes and goes — except perhaps coffee.

New York has popularized and perfected America's favorite caffeine fix, from good old-fashioned espresso to trendy spiced coffee. Here are the top five coffee shops you can't miss.

5. Birch

What started out as two friends' $10,000 investment is now a multimillion-dollar coffee shop with over 10 locations in New York City. Birch owes its huge success to its premium yet welcoming vibe and the best fresh-roasted cup in the City.

A regular cup of coffee starts at $3. Regulars recommend the cheddar chive scone, on the off chance that you're lucky enough to see it in the few minutes before it gets sold out. All of Birch's 10 locations are open daily from 7 a.m. to 8 p.m.

171 E 88th Street, New York, NY 10128

750 Columbus Avenue, New York, NY 10025

134 1/2 E 62nd Street, New York, NY 10065

40-37 23rd Street, Long Island City, NY 11101

432 3rd Avenue, New York, NY 10016

21 E 27th Street, New York, NY 10016

56 7th Avenue, New York, NY 10011

71 W Houston Street, New York, NY 10012

8 Spruce Street, New York, NY 10038

884 9th Avenue, New York, NY 10019

Phone: 212-686-1444
http://birchcoffee.com/

4. Little Collins

Buried among Midtown's popular coffee chains is Little Collins. This Australian-owned hidden gem steals people away with its chic decor, friendly service, and of course, outstanding coffee paired with its crown jewel, avocado smash.

Coffee starts at $4. Visit this quaint cafe at 667 Lexington Avenue, New York, NY 10022, from 7 a.m. to 5 p.m.

Phone: 212 -308-1969
http://www.littlecollinsnyc.com/

3. Hi-Collar

High-end Japanese coffee shop by day; exclusive beer and sake bar by night. The name Hi-Collar comes from the term hi-kara, meaning Japan's fascination and integration with Western and American concepts and culture. This coffee shop offers the Japanese take on American coffee. What's more, you have the option to pick your coffee beans and brewing technique.

Hi-Collar is located at 214 East 10th Street, New York, NY 10003. The cafe is open from 11 a.m. to 5 p.m., and the bar is open from 6 p.m. to 1 a.m.

Phone:212-777-7018
https://www.hi-collar.com/

2. Everyman Espresso

Everyman Espresso, true to its name, is for every man. The humble coffee shop doesn't dazzle you with flashy interiors and exotic food; instead, it keeps its head down and does its work. And you'll know they did a great job when you taste their old-fashioned espresso.

Everyman Espresso has three locations in New York. All are open daily from 7 a.m. to 7 p.m.

301 West Broadway, New York
136 E. 13th Street, New York
162 5th Avenue, Brooklyn, New York

http://www.everymanespresso.com/

1. Intelligentsia Coffee

This high-end cafe is situated at the lobby of High Line Hotel. It is only a few steps away from High Line, Chelsea Market, and David Zwirner Gallery.

On top of its excellent location, this coffee shop offers artisanal single-origin, daily-roasted fresh brews. Its outdoor seating allows you to take a gander at the view of the Hudson River.

Drop by at 180 10th Avenue at 20th Street New York, New York 10011, from 7 a.m. to 6 p.m. A nice, fresh cup of Intelligentsia coffee will be waiting for you.

Phone: 212-933-9736
https://www.intelligentsiacoffee.com/

10

Bars

Hole-in-the-walls, dive bars, authentic Irish pubs, speakeasies, karaokes — the city has it all.

End a packed day with friends and strangers, and have a drink or two. Here are New York's top five bars.

5. Attaboy

Ask, and you shall receive. Attaboy has no menus and no cocktail list. Instead, their talented team of bartenders asks your usual taste and preferences, and serves you an innovative twist on your drink of choice.

Attaboy is a speakeasy, meaning half the fun is finding its secret entrance. When you do manage to find the doorman, you'll be greeted with a laid-back atmosphere great for drinks with a small group of friends.

You can find Attaboy at 134 Eldridge Street, New York, NY 10002. The bar is open every day from 6 p.m. to 4 a.m.

http://attaboy.us/nyc/

4. The Spotted Pig

The Spotted Pig is a quirky, no-reservations gastropub in Greenwich. Despite not implementing a reservation system, the Spotted Pig offers relatively short wait times and adequate seating. The adventure begins when you're seated in your booth. Order your choice of burger with a side of shoestring fries, and wash it down with a pint of beer.

The Spotted Pig doesn't fall prey to the New York tendency to stand out to set itself apart from the norm. They just serve you warm food with cold beer, and let the gastronomic experience speak for itself.

The Spotted Pig is located at 314 W 11th Street, New York, NY 10014. It is open every day from 12 p.m. to 5 p.m., and 5:30 p.m. to 2 a.m.

Phone: 212-620-0393
https://www.thespottedpig.com

3. Copper & Oak

New York isn't just all beers and cocktails, it can be scotch and whiskey, too. Copper & Oak has a fine staff of bartenders willing to enthuse you with their whiskey expertise, ensuring happy hour is as enjoyable (and informative!) as possible.

You can find Copper & Oak at 157 Allen Street, New York, NY 10002. The bar is open from 5 p.m. to 1 a.m. Tuesdays to Saturdays and 2 p.m. to 10 p.m. on Sundays.

Phone: 212-460-5546
http://www.copperandoak.com/

2. Barcade

In 2004, Barcade was just four friends with a love for craft beer and retro arcade games. Fast-forward to 2018, and the bar-slash-arcade is now a multimillion-dollar bar chain with five locations across the five boroughs.

Get a pint of their famous craft beer, then prepare your quarters and play vintage games like Donkey Kong, Pac Man, and Dig Dug. Visit Barcade in its original Williamsburg location, 388 Union Avenue, Brooklyn, NY 11211. It is open from 4 p.m. to 4 a.m. on weekdays and 12 p.m. to 4 a.m. on weekends.

Phone: +1 718-302-6464
https://barcadebrooklyn.com/

1. Bar SixtyFive

Partake in the best of what New York has to offer. This cocktail lounge is the highest terrace bar in the city, located at the 65th floor of the Rockefeller Plaza.

The prices are sky-high, but some things are more important the money. At the very least, their excellent cocktails take the sting out of the prices. You'll also be comforted by the magnificent 360-degree view of New York City, and that is something you can't put a price on.

Bar SixtyFive is in Rainbow Room, 30 Rockefeller Plaza, 65th Floor, New York, NY 10112. It is open from 5 p.m. to 12 a.m. Reservations are recommended.

Phone: 212-632-5000

https://rainbowroom.com/bar-sixty-five/

11

Nightclubs

If you're looking for a night of drinking, dancing, and partying, you're in luck. The city that never sleeps, never does so for a reason. Swing your way through New York's top five nightclubs.

5. The Box

The doorman might need a little convincing, but once you get past those doors, the rest of the night is smooth-sailing. The Box is one of the most premier locations in New York for a little theatre, music, and burlesque dancing.

The erotic nightclub is famous for being in the hit TV series "Gossip Girl." In real life, The Box doesn't disappoint; it lives up to the glitz and glamour of the elites of the Upper East Side. So sit back, order a drink, and enjoy the show.

Visit The Box at 189 Chrystie Street, New York, NY 10002. It is open from 11 p.m. to 4 p.m., Tuesdays to Saturdays.

Phone: +1 212-982-9301
http://www.theboxnyc.com/

4. PH-D

This high-end spot offers live DJs, a rooftop view of Manhattan, and a likely chance of celeb-spotting. PH-D's crowd is mostly the rich and famous, which makes entrance exclusive. Guests of the Dream Downtown Hotel enjoy unlimited access, but others might need to sneak a tip the doorman.

PH-D Lounge is located at Dream Downtown Hotel, 355 W 16th Street, New York, NY 10011. It is open every day from 5 p.m. to 4 a.m.

Phone: +1 212-229-2511
http://phdlounge.com/

3. Comedy Cellar

Comedy Cellar might not have the allure of other nightclubs in this list, but it certainly has grit and character. This is for the stand-up fans — Comedy Central is a comedy club first and a nightclub second. Famous comedians like Amy Schumer, Dave Attell, and Todd Barry found their start in this very club, so you might expect to see some familiar faces, too.

You can find Comedy Central at 1267, 117 Macdougal Street, New York, NY 10012. It is open every day from 11 a.m. to 3 a.m.

Phone: +1 212-254-3480
https://www.comedycellar.com/

2. Output

New York can be a new city where nobody knows you and you can be someone new. Output allows you exactly that — in this neon-lit electronica dance club, all of your inhibitions are stripped away and are replaced with the need to move and groove to the music.

Drinks are on the expensive side, but the dance floor can easily accommodate 500 people. Celebrity DJs like Skrillex and John Digweed also regularly play at this venue. Visit Output at 74 Wythe Avenue, Brooklyn, NY 11249. It is open from 10 p.m. to 4 a.m., Wednesdays to Sundays.

Phone:
http://outputclub.com/

1. House of Yes

The award for New York's wildest nightclub goes to House of Yes. Every night, this nightclub morphs into something different — Ancient Aliens party one day, Endless Summer Pool party the next. Prepare for eclectic drinks, vogue costumes, and all-out performances. In this club, anything can happen — all-night dance parties, mid-air acrobats, and burlesque dancers. You just have to say yes.

House of Yes is located at 2 Wyckoff Avenue, Brooklyn, NY 11237. It is open Wednesdays to Sundays, from 7 p.m. to 4 a.m.

Phone: +1 718-675-6290
https://houseofyes.org/

12

Only in New York

What makes a city is its people. The city results from the densely packed amalgamation of immigrants from all over the world who brought bits and pieces of their home — unique, colorful bits and pieces interacting with other unique, colorful bits and pieces, causing an explosion of culture, tradition, and history. In many ways, New York is a fast-paced modernized microcosm of the world.

All New Yorkers believe that they live in the greatest city in the world, and here are seven reasons why they're right.

Entertainment. The city is dripping with creativity, passion, and self-expression. It's good to know that even in a fast-paced city, people stop to smell the flowers. Performance art, live music, comedy improv, and even flash mob dances liven up the streets of New York City.

Pizza is the heritage of Italian-American immigrants. New York-style pizza comes in large slices with thin crusts, and is traditionally eaten by folding the slices vertically. You've never had pizza unless you've had pizza in New York, so grab a slice or two before you leave. The best pizza places in New York are Lombardi's, Di Fara, and Patsy's Pizzeria.

Lombardi's

32 Spring Street , New York, NY 10012
Open every day from 11:30 a.m. to 11 p.m.

http://www.firstpizza.com/

Di Fara

1424 Avenue J, Brooklyn, NY 11230
Open Tuesday to Sunday, 12 p.m. to 8 p.m.
https://www.difarapizzamenu.com/

Patsy's Pizzeria

2287 1st Avenue, New York, NY 10035
Open every day from 11 a.m. to 12 a.m.
http://www.thepatsyspizza.com/

Hot dogs. Not all hot dogs are created equal. New York hot dogs, for example, give a mouth-watering twist to the simple dog in a bun. For the best hot dogs in the city, head on to Katz's Delicatessen, Crif Dogs, Gray's Papaya, and The Nomad Bar. Or, considering the abundance of hot dog carts in New York, simply walk over to any corner with $2 in hand, buy a hotdog, and ask for extra mustard and sauerkraut.

Katz's Delicatessen

205 E Houston Street, New York, NY 10002
Open every day from 8 a.m. to 10:45 p.m.
https://www.katzsdelicatessen.com/

Crif Dogs

113 St Marks Pl, New York, NY 10009
Open every day from 12 p.m. to 2 a.m.
http://www.crifdogs.com/

Gray's Papaya

2090 Broadway, New York, NY 10023, USA
Open 24 hours every day
http://grayspapaya.nyc/

The NoMad Bar

10 W 28th Street, Broadway and, W 28th St, New York, NY 10016
Open 24 hours every day
https://www.thenomadhotel.com

Chinatown gives a bite-sized taste of its mother country. Tourists flock to Chinatown for its exotic restaurants, gift and souvenir shops, food markets, karaoke, and Chinese New Year celebrations. Make sure to take a stroll down Doyers Street, sample the dumplings, get your fortune told, and take home a kitschy souvenir.

Weird, quirky museums. New York is artsy, creative, humorous, and whimsical; of course there's no shortage of unusual and niche museums. New York's roster includes the Museum of Food and Drink, Mmuseumm, and Museum of Sex.

Museum of Food and Drink

62 Bayard Street, Brooklyn, NY 11222
Open Friday to Sunday, 12 p.m. to 6 p.m.
https://www.mofad.org/

Mmuseumm

4 Cortlandt Alley, New York, NY 10013
Open Saturday and Sunday, 12 p.m. to 6 p.m.
http://www.mmuseumm.com/

Museum of Sex

233 5th Avenue, New York, NY 10016
Open daily from 10:30 a.m. to 10 p.m.
https://www.museumofsex.com/

Speakeasies. New York loves history, drinking, and 20s aesthetics — which is why speakeasies are making a comeback. In fact, there are more hidden bars now than there were during the Prohibition era.

There's a thrill from drinking and dancing in clandestine bars — and you best believe that New York can deliver. The best secret bars in New York are Beauty and Essex, The Back Room, and Please Don't Tell.

Beauty & Essex

146 Essex Street, New York, NY 10002
Open from 5 p.m. to 12 a.m. on weekdays, 11:30 a.m. to 3 p.m. and 5 p.m. to 12 a.m. on weekends
http://beautyandessex.com/

The Back Room

102 Norfolk Street, New York, NY 10002
Open every day from 7:30 p.m. to 3 a.m.

http://www.backroomnyc.com/

Please Don't Tell

113 St Marks Pl, New York, NY 10009
Open every day from 6 p.m. to 2 a.m.
http://www.pdtnyc.com/

LGBT culture. On the eve of June 28, 1969, the LGBT resistance reached a boiling point and crystallized, taking the form of a shot glass. A bar in Greenwich Village named Stonewall Inn was violently raided and people were arrested on charges of solicitation of homosexual relations and public indecency.

Marsha P. Johnson, a black transgender woman, cried, "I got my civil rights!" In anger, she threw a shot glass, breaking a mirror, and a riot ensued. Over 500 people rioted in protest, outnumbering the police. That night, the LGBT community was realized, and New York became the epicenter of the resistance. The anniversary of the Stonewall Riots marked the first Pride March, which was held in New York.

Today, New York has one of the largest and most vibrant LGBT communities. LGBT activities include visiting the still-standing Stonewall Inn, joining the Pride Parade, partying in gay and lesbian bars, and attending the New York Lesbian, Gay, Bisexual, and Transgender Film Festival.

The Stonewall Inn
53 Christopher Street, New York, NY 10014
Open every day from 2 p.m. to 4 a.m.
https://thestonewallinnnyc.com/

13

Safety Tips

New York Police

Despite popular belief, crime in New York has significantly and steadily gone down since 1991. In 2017, it was ranked the safest major city in the US. Still, minor crimes and accidents are common. Keep in mind the following tips for a safe trip.

Before leaving for New York, inform your bank, especially when you're planning to use a debit or credit card. If your bank sees suspicious activity in your card (i.e. sudden overseas or out-of-state purchases), they can temporarily freeze your account.

Pack a distinct, recognizable, clearly labeled luggage to avoid getting held up at the airport. Never let your belongings out of your sight.

Take a cab at the airport and go directly to your hotel. Once in a cab, look for the medallion number and ID number. Write it down in case of accidents.

Leave important documents in a hotel room safe and carry only what's necessary for the day.

Wearing I-heart-NY shirts makes you an obvious tourist, which makes you an obvious target. Opt for sensible clothing.

New York is a walkable city, but always be aware of your surroundings. Keep an eye out for cars and cyclists.

As a rule of thumb, take great caution in interacting with strangers, especially those who offer to carry your bags or give you a ride.

Emergency Number New York: 911

14

Recommended Travel Itinerary

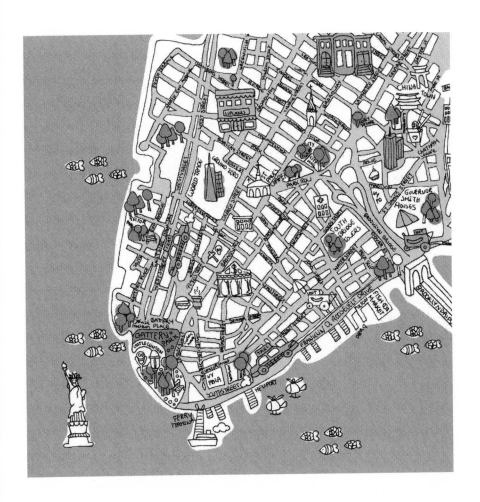

Day 1

Times Square

Start your trip with a bang. The iconic Times Square is where New York's tourists come to be dazzled. Shopaholics would not be disappointed by the abundance of shops in Times Square — Grand Slam New York, Disney Store, and Hershey's, to name a few. Grab a quick bite at the famous Hard Rock Cafe; you'll need the energy.

Rockefeller Center

Ten minutes away from Times Square is Rockefeller Center, home of the world-famous skating rink, Radio City Music Hall, and Top of the Rock Observation Deck. If you haven't yet bought it online, you can purchase the New York Pass here. It is an all-access pass to over 100 attractions in New York. For 3 days, the pass costs $199 for adults and $154 for senior citizens.

Rockefeller Center

Museum-Hopping

Only in New York would you have such easy access to the world's most famous museums. Four blocks away from Rockefeller is the Museum of Modern Art. MoMA has over 200,000 artworks on contemporary art, making it the epicenter of the modern art movement.

Next up is the Metropolitan Museum of Art. As it is America's largest art museum, don't expect to see everything. Grab a map and view the highlights — Egyptian Art, American Wing, European Sculpture and Decorative Arts, Medieval Art, Robert Lehman Collection, and Greek and Roman Art. Then, head on to Solomon R. Guggenheim Museum, which features modern and post-modern art inside its stylish, avant-garde spiral architecture.

Museum-hopping can take most of the day (and most of your energy).

Where better to take a break than at Central Park?

Central Park

Just across the street from the last museum is the perfect spot for resting, effortless sightseeing, and snacking. Central Park offers a host of entertainment options, too — a zoo, carousel, boat rental, and puppet shows.

Day 2

Lower Manhattan

One World Observatory is located at the 100th to 102nd floor of the One World Trade Center. Visit the observatory first thing in the morning to see the city from the highest skyscraper in New York. The elevator ride alone is breathtaking, not to mention the view 541m from the ground.

One World Trade Center

Right in front is the September 11 Memorial. Take a moment to visit Reflecting Absence, a memorial structure commemorating the lives lost to the horrific terrorist attack.

Next, visit Wall Street, New York's financial district. Wall Street is more than just premier, intimidating skyscrapers. A tour of the area can introduce you to the National Museum of the American Indian, Charging Bull, Fearless Girl, and Stone Street.

Battery Park

Head south and you'll be in Battery Park, a 25-acre park facing the harbor. The battery is a tranquil recreational park containing many monuments and memorials, like Fritz Koenig's The Sphere and the Hope Garden.

The former is initially located in front of the World Trade Center, where it served as a symbol of the importance of trade to world peace.

Battery Park

The sculpture sustained visible damage during the 9/11 attack; then it was relocated to The Battery.The dents and holes of The Sphere were never repaired on purpose, because Koenig thought that it was a monument to resilience.

The latter, on the other hand, is a memorial garden. The 100,000 wild roses that bloom in Hope Garden is a way to remember the lives lost in the AIDS crisis of the 1960s.

Head on to the opposite side and you'll see the Battery Park Terminal, where you can ride a ferry, sightseeing boat, or water taxi to Ellis Island and the Statue of Liberty.

Statue of Liberty

You've seen it in photos, you've seen it from afar, but nothing can truly prepare you from the moment you realize just how impressive the Statue of Liberty is.

In 1886, the 46-meter-high monument was the first sight that welcomed immigrants coming to America through Ellis Island. This sentiment was apt; after all, inscribed in the statue is the famous poem that lends a helping hand to the poor, sick, and weary. To the newcomers, the statue promises a better land than the one that they had left.

If you intend to visit the crown, it is best to book a tour beforehand. The benefits of pre-booking include guided tours, free transportation, guaranteed protection from scams, and in some cases, a trip to Ellis Island.

Ellis Island served as New York's immigration center during the 1880s, welcoming over 12 million immigrants in the span of 62 years. The immigration station is now a museum. Ellis Island Museum is a token of remembrance and gratitude for the immigrants who came to the country with nothing except the clothes on their backs, but pulled themselves up by the bootstraps and contributed to building the new land.

Day 3

Chelsea

Flea markets? Check. Art galleries? Check. Nightlife? Check. Chelsea is the neighborhood that caters to every kind of tourist. Visit the High Line, a train railway turned miniature aboveground eco-park with a scenic view of New York and the Hudson River. Then a defunct train station, it's now a tourist attraction that attracts 5 million visitors annually. If you're staying somewhere you can cook, visit the Chelsea Market for fresh produce.

Greenwich Village

Jimi Hendrix. Bob Dylan. Jon Stewart. Marsha P. Johnson. What they all have in common is that they all found their start in Greenwich Village. The village, as it's called by locals, is a haven for creativity. Make sure to drop by Washington Square Park for public performance art, then across the street to Comedy Cellar for hilarious stand-up.

Chinatown

Chinatown

Take a walk down the vibrant Motts, Pell, and Doyes Streets and see the best of what Chinatown has to offer. There is no shortage of bizarre food and cheap clothes, jewelry, and bags. Vegetarians should try the neighborhood's hidden gem, the Vegetarian Dim Sum House.

Brooklyn Bridge

An exciting, eventful trip deserves a peaceful ending. Ride the 4, 5, 6 trains to Brooklyn Bridge stop, and head over to the Brooklyn Bridge. You can walk from Manhattan to Brooklyn in 30 minutes; less if you choose to bike. If you can, visit the bridge just before sunset. Take a minute and enjoy the view of New York, Brooklyn, and the Statue of Liberty in all of its glorious entirety.

Brooklyn Bridge

15

Conclusion

I'd like to thank you and congratulate you for transiting my lines from start to finish.

I hope this book was able to help you to prepare for your New York trip! Knowing what to expect doesn't lessen the excitement; rather, it heightens it.

Every city exists in three dimensions — in its history, its appearance, and its ideals. Learning about a city's context allows you to enjoy it past its aesthetics. New York, in particular, has a dazzlingly distracting aesthetic. Its facade can easily tempt you to only look at it from one dimension. But knowing its history and its ideals makes you understand it, from root to flower, and that understanding allows you to genuinely engage with it.

I hope this book helps you see New York City in three dimensions. I hope that because of this book, you make the transition from tourist to traveler.

The next step is to take that leap of faith. Plan your trip, pack your bags, and set off. The bright lights of the big city await.

I wish you the best of luck!

16

Thank You

I want to thank you for reading this book! I sincerely hope that you received value from it!

If you received value from this book, I want to ask you for a favour .Would you be kind enough to leave a review for this book on Amazon?

Maps

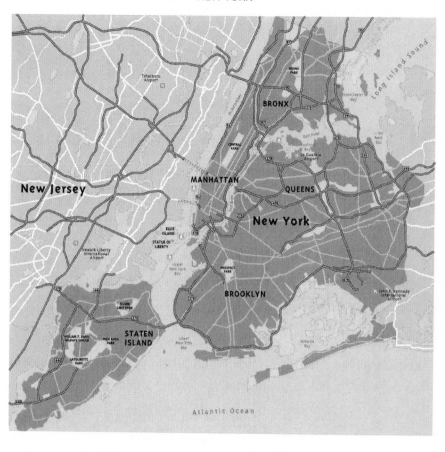

Manhattan

Staten Island

Brooklyn

Queens

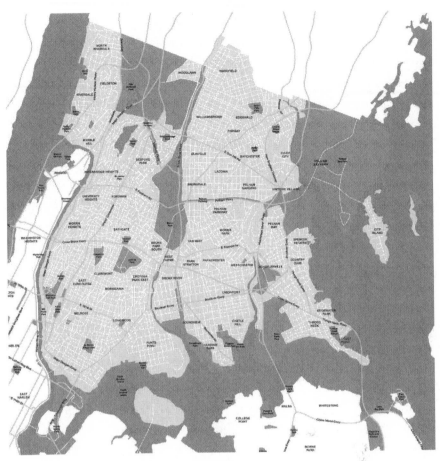

Bronx

This document is geared towards providing exact and reliable information in regards to the topic and issue covered. The publication is sold with the idea that the publisher is not required to render accounting, officially permitted, or otherwise, qualified services. If advice is necessary, legal or professional, a practiced individual in the profession should be ordered.

- From a Declaration of Principles which was accepted and approved equally by a Committee of the American Bar Association and a Committee of Publishers and Associations.

In no way is it legal to reproduce, duplicate, or transmit any part of this document in either electronic means or in printed format. Recording of this publication is strictly prohibited and any storage of this document is not allowed unless with written permission from the publisher. All rights reserved.

The information provided herein is stated to be truthful and consistent, in that any liability, in terms of inattention or otherwise, by any usage or abuse of any policies, processes, or directions contained within is the solitary and utter responsibility of the recipient reader. Under no circumstances will any legal responsibility or blame be held against the publisher for any reparation, damages, or monetary loss due to the information herein, either directly or indirectly.

Respective authors own all copyrights not held by the publisher.

The information herein is offered for informational purposes solely, and is universal as so. The presentation of the information is without contract or any type of guarantee assurance.

The trademarks that are used are without any consent, and the publication of the trademark is without permission or backing by the trademark owner. All trademarks and brands within this book are for clarifying purposes only and are the owned by the owners themselves, not affiliated with this document.